T0270490

Addressing Stressors for National Guard Personnel

Insights From Leadership

CHAITRA M. HARDISON, DANIEL B. GINSBERG

Prepared for the Office of the Secretary of Defense
Approved for public release; distribution is unlimited.

RAND NATIONAL DEFENSE RESEARCH INSTITUTE

For more information on this publication, visit **www.rand.org/t/RRA2052-1**

About RAND

The RAND Corporation is a research organization that develops solutions to public policy challenges to help make communities throughout the world safer and more secure, healthier and more prosperous. RAND is nonprofit, nonpartisan, and committed to the public interest. To learn more about RAND, visit www.rand.org.

Research Integrity

Our mission to help improve policy and decisionmaking through research and analysis is enabled through our core values of quality and objectivity and our unwavering commitment to the highest level of integrity and ethical behavior. To help ensure our research and analysis are rigorous, objective, and nonpartisan, we subject our research publications to a robust and exacting quality-assurance process; avoid both the appearance and reality of financial and other conflicts of interest through staff training, project screening, and a policy of mandatory disclosure; and pursue transparency in our research engagements through our commitment to the open publication of our research findings and recommendations, disclosure of the source of funding of published research, and policies to ensure intellectual independence. For more information, visit www.rand.org/about/research-integrity.

RAND's publications do not necessarily reflect the opinions of its research clients and sponsors.

Cover: U.S. Air National Guard photo by Master Sgt. David Kujawa.

About This Report

The National Guard serves as a reserve component of the armed services and military force under control of the 54 States, Territories, and the District of Columbia of the United States. Since the drawdown from Afghanistan that began in 2020, the pace of National Guard operations overseas has declined. However, domestic demands seem to have been much higher than in past decades, with the Department of Defense (DoD) and the states intensively tasking the National Guard (its Air and Army components) to respond to the coronavirus disease 2019 (COVID-19) pandemic, civil unrest, border operations, and natural disasters. This high demand for National Guard support of domestic operations has raised concerns about potential impacts for Guard members and their families, as well as a range of personnel management challenges (retention, recruiting) for the National Guard Bureau (NGB) force. For this report, we held interviews with senior leaders in the National Guard, within both the NGB and the states, to lay out a starting picture of the Guard's recent mission demands, identify the challenges that the pace of operations has created for Guard members and their families, and explore what service and support programs are in place to address these challenges. The study interviews took place from summer 2022 through the beginning of 2023.

The research reported here completed in September 2023 and underwent security review with the sponsor and the Defense Office of Prepublicaiton and Security Review before public release.

RAND National Security Research Division

This research was conducted within the Personnel, Readiness, and Health (PRH) Program of the RAND National Security Research Division (NSRD), which operates the RAND National Defense Research Institute (NDRI), a federally funded research and development center (FFRDC) sponsored by the Office of the Secretary of Defense, the Joint Staff, the Unified Combatant Commands, the Navy, the Marine Corps, the defense agencies, and the defense intelligence enterprise. This research was made possible by NDRI exploratory research funding that was provided through the FFRDC contract and approved by NDRI's primary sponsor.

For more information on the RAND Personnel, Readiness, and Health Program see www.rand/org/nsrd/prh or contact the director (contact information is provided on the webpage).

Acknowledgments

We would first like to acknowledge Major General Giselle M. Wilz (Director of Staff, NGB), who served as our primary NGB contact for the study and our NGB senior leader advocate for the work. Having her full support, as well as her insights and guidance, over the course of the project was invaluable. We would also like to thank Lt Col Mario A. (Tony) Pena (U.S. Air Force) of the NGB, who served as our project point of contact. He was instrumental in coordinating our discussions with NGB senior leaders and in tracking down a wide range of internal briefings and documentation for us to review over the course of the study.

We would also like to acknowledge our DoD contract officer sponsors, who recognized a need to explore NGB-specific stressor issues further, supported our research idea, and agreed to fund the study.

Inside RAND, we would like to thank Barbara Bicksler, who offered expert communication and writing assistance on our report drafts and on sponsor briefings. We also thank our reviewer Shirley M. Ross, who provided thoughtful comments on early drafts of this report. Molly F. McIntosh, Director of the Personnel, Readiness, and Health program, provided invaluable comments on the report.

Lastly, we would like to express our sincerest gratitude to all our senior leader interview participants who graciously offered their time and insights to the study.

Summary

The National Guard is a dual-missioned armed force available to conduct federal missions as a component of the U.S. Army and U.S. Air Force and state missions under the control of governors. Since the drawdown from Afghanistan that began in 2020, the pace of National Guard overseas operations as a key organization in the Department of Defense (DoD) has declined, though the Guard maintains a relatively intense mission load. However, domestic demands seem to have been much higher than in past decades, with DoD and the states intensively tasking the National Guard (its Air and Army components) to respond to the coronavirus disease 2019 (COVID-19) pandemic, civil unrest, border operations, and natural disasters.

This high demand for National Guard support of domestic operations has raised concerns about potential impacts for Guard members and their families and about the potential for a range of personnel management challenges (retention, recruiting) for the National Guard. In this report, we lay out a picture of the Guard's recent mission demands, identify the challenges that the pace of operations has created for Guard members and their families, and explore what service and support programs are in place to address these challenges.

Approach

This project was conceived as a small exploratory effort to help generate ideas and identify areas that might benefit from a larger, follow-on research effort. With this scope and intent in mind, to explore the above research questions, we took a three-pronged approach that consisted of reviewing publicly available articles and reports, holding interviews with National Guard senior leader stakeholders and subject-matter experts (SMEs), and reviewing existing internal National Guard documents provided to us by our interviewees.

Although the articles, reports, and documents we reviewed provided useful background and touched on recent stressors in the National Guard workforce, in most cases they did not provide much detail. As a result, the bulk of our findings were derived from the details we uncovered through our interviews.

There were two categories of interviewees we invited to participate. The first included senior leader stakeholders and SMEs (e.g., directorate heads and other key officials) from within the Joint Staff of the National Guard Bureau (NGB). These key senior leader stakeholders and SMEs were identified by the Office of the Director of Staff within the NGB, which made introductions to the key leaders and recommended that we include them as participants. The second category included State Adjutants General who were identified as potentially having important insights by some of the senior leader stakeholders and SMEs. In total, we held 12 interviews (eight from the NGB headquarters offices and four with Adjutants General). Interviews were conducted from summer 2022 through the beginning of 2023.

Key Findings

Leaders offered a variety of discussion points about stressors in the workplace. One discussion point was the *pace of operations*. While the drawdown in Afghanistan has led to a reduction in the number of federal Title 10 missions, the National Guard sustains a high operational tempo, taking on numerous missions that reflect its role as an integral operational reserve to the U.S. Air Force and the U.S. Army. A notable increase in domestic missions, which are requested under Federal Title 32 and Title 10 and requested by the state, has been driven by natural disaster response, civil unrest, and requests to supplement overwhelmed social services. This has led to an increased personnel tempo (PERSTEMPO) for some personnel. Leaders explained that family separations and the bureaucratic challenges that come from switching among authorized duty statuses adds considerable stress on Guard members. They also talked about uncertainty as a stressor associated with the new pace of operations and the fact that some types of operations are more stressful than others.

Personnel fundamentals (recruiting, retention, and manpower requirements) were discussed as well. Leaders noted that recruiting is a problem, but they also said the issue is not unique to the National Guard. They said that retention does not seem to be a problem so far, yet they are concerned about the future. With respect to manpower requirements, leaders noted a lack of visibility regarding the numbers of personnel needed or utilized at the state level, but they also noted that some states are believed to be stretched thin.

Leaders talked about how *ancillary training and other work demands* also impact stress and exacerbate the PERSTEMPO issues. They noted that atrophying skills were a potential concern given the high pace of operations and, as a result, limited time for training. They also explained that although automated and self-paced trainings are generally good, there are also internet access issues. Leaders also talked about the role of bureaucracy, noting that administrative hurdles frequently create more work and detract from the mission.

Several interviewees mentioned the role of various *social and lifestyle considerations*. One issue they mentioned was that increased disconnectedness was a concern. Although many people enjoy the remote work lifestyle and want more of it, leaders noted that it meant that there were fewer opportunities for interpersonal connections. Some also believe that guard members may be more dispersed than in the past, living farther from their units and assignments. Because of the dispersion of personnel and increased remote work, leaders expressed concern that support networks were missing. In addition, they noted that people were traveling farther for drilling, leading to an increased commute burden. Leaders also noted that people living in remote locations (far from bases and urban centers) were more likely to have reduced access to services.

Lastly, *health care* and *child care* were discussed as sources of stress for many guard members. In particular, interviewees talked about lacking access to health care providers in general. According to the senior leaders we interviewed, few doctors accept DoD's military health insurance program, TRICARE, and some accept only a few patients under TRICARE. Access to specialists is limited in remote locations, and mental health care is particularly hard to find. Guard leaders mentioned how the transition across duty statuses causes issues for health care—coverage changes by status, transitioning comes with paperwork burdens and delays in coverage, and there are issues with continuity of care. With respect to child care, Guard leaders noted that it is hard to find weekend care in general, and it is also difficult when child care needs are infrequent (e.g., one Saturday a month), irregular, or unpredictable (e.g., only on Monday, Tuesday and Wednesday, or some weeks and not other weeks). They also talked about problems transitioning across statuses, the cost of care, and limitations in what was available in remote locations.

Recommendations

This report's description of the variety of issues facing the National Guard is an important foundational step. This information can help leaders see the full variety of issues that they likely need to address and consider which of them to prioritize. It also can help illustrate the complexity of these stressors and why making policy changes in one area might not be enough. However, this exploration of issues cannot define the specific policy solutions that are needed in any given area. Identifying detailed solutions would require deep dives into individual topics, which were beyond the scope of this limited, exploratory report.

With this in mind, we recommend that the National Guard conduct targeted research on the following key topics that could benefit from additional data collection and exploration:

- Workforce stress in the National Guard population
  - Confirm whether the broader workforce's views on top stressors are consistent with leadership's understanding of the issues.
  - Conduct follow-on focus groups and surveys with the broader workforce to explore their views on stressors.
  - Gather longitudinal data on the impacts of the full range of stress prevention and mitigation programs on workforce stressors.

- Improving service member access to care and well-being services and supports
  - Address child care access as a stressor.
  - Identify pros and cons of solutions to address the health care access issues and gaps in coverage.
  - Understand and address interpersonal disconnectedness.

- Tracking and mitigating PERSTEMPO
  - Better track and account for state-workload PERSTEMPO stressors.
  - Explore whether existing processes for defining National Guard manpower requirements (at both the state and federal level) are capturing and addressing fluctuations in workload demands.

Lastly, it is worth noting that studies on some of these topics are already underway. For example, DoD has commissioned a congressionally mandated study of ways to improve health care access, and the NGB is piloting a new child care program in six states. In addition, there are efforts underway to enact reforms to status changes that might help reduce some of the stressors that leaders identified. Nevertheless, more work on these topics could still be beneficial and help round out these other efforts.

Contents

Tables

Introduction

The National Guard serves as a statutory component of the U.S. Army and the U.S. Air Force, as well as a state force available for domestic missions under the control of the nation's governors. Since the drawdown from Afghanistan that began in 2020, the pace of National Guard operations overseas has declined, though the Guard continues to conduct intensive missions alongside its active-component counterparts. However, domestic demands seem to be much higher than in past decades, with the Department of Defense (DoD) and the states intensively tasking the National Guard to respond to the coronavirus disease 2019 (COVID-19) pandemic, civil unrest, border operations, and natural disasters.

This high demand for National Guard support of domestic operations, along with sustained federal missions, has raised concerns about potential impacts for Guard members and their families and about the potential for a variety of personnel management challenges (retention, recruiting) for the National Guard (Knowles and Demirjian, 2022; Nierenberg 2022). In this report, we lay out a picture of the Guard's recent mission demands, identify the challenges that the pace of operations has created for Guard members and their families, and explore what service and support programs are in place to address these challenges.

Objectives and Approach

This study is an exploratory first step in systematically identifying stressors facing the National Guard since the start of 2020. We explored the following research questions:

- Have recent mission demands increased relative to prior years? If so, are those increased demands likely to continue?
- What are some of the challenges that the recent pace of operations has created for Guard members and their families?
- Are there other stressors in addition to the pace of operations?
- What service and support programs are designed to address these challenges?
- How are National Guard leaders monitoring operations and stress on personnel?

It is important to note that our project was resourced to serve as a first look at these topics only. It was funded as a small initial effort to help generate ideas and identify areas that might benefit from more targeted, follow-on research efforts. We therefore view it as a useful exploratory effort to systematically capture and centrally document the strategic issues, concerns, and hypotheses that leaders, subject-matter experts (SMEs), and stakeholders identified individually. The goal was to help DoD and National Guard leadership identify areas in which further exploration could be valuable for informing future resourcing decisions.

With this scope and intent in mind, to explore the above research questions, we took a three-pronged approach that consisted of the following:

1. Reviewing publicly available articles and reports
2. Holding interviews with National Guard senior leader stakeholders and SMEs
3. Reviewing existing internal National Guard documents provided to us by our interviewees.

Internal documents provided to us by interviewees served as useful background for our discussions. We also found publicly available articles that touched on concerns about recent stressors in the National Guard. These provided a few useful insights that are interspersed throughout our report where relevant. However, the bulk of the details and specifics we sought were identified through our interviews. For that reason, we have focused our findings primarily on the interview results, which we discuss in the remainder of this report.

Our goal for the interviews was to gather input and insights from National Guard leaders who would be considered relevant stakeholders or SMEs based on their office's area of primary responsibility. With this in mind, we identified several National Guard Bureau (NGB) Headquarters offices responsible for key personnel domains that might be affected by or have visibility into the full range of workforce stressors (e.g., the J1, J3, and J5 offices; the NGB Surgeon General's office) and invited key senior leaders and SMEs from across these relevant offices to participate. The Office of the Director of Staff of the NGB made introductions and assisted with scheduling interviews. We also recognized that soliciting insights from some state-level National Guard leaders—specifically The Adjutants General (TAGs)—would be especially important as well, so we invited several TAGs to participate. Some of the TAGs we invited were from states or territories where the populations are smaller, more rural, and more dispersed; others were from key states or territories known to have had high demands placed on them in recent years. In total, we held 12 interviews. Eight were with leaders or SMEs from across the NGB headquarters offices, and four were with TAGs. Interviews were conducted from summer 2022 through the beginning of 2023.

Why Is It Important for Organizations to Understand and Address Their Unique Workplace Stressors?

Stress is a normal part of life and unavoidable in the workplace. While some stress can be beneficial and even necessary to motivate action or performance, it is well established that too much stress and chronic stress can lead to many negative outcomes for employers and their employees. The health care cost alone can be substantial. For example, Goh, Pfeffer, and Zenios (2016) have estimated that workplace stress costs the United States well over $170 billion in health care annually. Workforce stress can take a major toll on organizations in many other ways (e.g., reduced productivity, absences, turnover, other undesirable work behaviors), which we elaborate on below. Organizations should be on the lookout for problematic sources of stress and take steps to address them or mitigate them when possible.[1]

Stress can be influenced by a wide array of factors, all of which must be taken into consideration if an organization wants to reduce stress levels in the workforce. Existing research on workplace stress and dissatisfaction provides valuable insights into the types of factors that need to be examined. Hardison et al. (2014) provides an in-depth summary of the various topics that have been studied in the research literature, which helps explain why an organization such as the National Guard should be concerned with these matters.

As explained in that report, research on stress and dissatisfaction in the workplace identifies three broad topics to consider: (1) factors that affect well-being and attitudes in the workplace; (2) types of well-being, attitudes, and perceptions that hold significance; and (3) the consequences of well-being and attitudes for both organizations and individuals. Table 1.1 presents a variety of factors falling under each topic area. As illustrated in the table, numerous stressors and other relevant workplace, environmental, and individual factors have been recognized as affecting psychological and physical well-being, as well as important workplace attitudes.

For instance, *work and organizational characteristics*, such as skill variety, task identity, job feedback, and job enrichment have been found to correlate with employee satisfaction and motivation. Work hours, work demands, and work intensity can lead to exhaustion and burnout and ultimately have profound impacts on health and well-being. Organizational structure, climate, and culture are additional elements that can influence stress levels experienced by workers and their responses to stress. Workplace norms, for instance, can either generate tension and stress or act as psychological buffers. The level of support or conflict experienced in interactions with others within the organization can also affect psychological well-being. Evaluation and reward systems within the workplace contribute to employee motivation and satisfaction.

Environmental characteristics, such as commuting time, can also have implications for health and well-being. *Personal characteristics* play a role in the relationship between stress, attitudes, and perceptions in the workplace. Such factors as family demands, work-family conflict, and child care needs can impact these dynamics. Personality and temperament are critical factors driving workplace stress and can influence how individuals cope with stress in their work environment.

---

[1] The importance of addressing workplace stress is discussed in many places. For some examples, see Colligan and Higgins (2006), Hardison et al. (2014), Hardison et al. (2017), Avey, Luthans, and Jensen (2009), Edú-Valsania, Laguía, and Moriano (2022).

TABLE 1.1

Factors to Consider When Addressing Workplace Stress and Dissatisfaction

Factors That Affect Workplace Well-Being and Attitudes	Types of Well-Being, Attitudes, and Perceptions That Matter in the Workplace	Consequences for Organizations and Individuals
Work and Organizational Characteristics	*Well-Being*	*Organizational Consequences*

• Work hours—amount and schedule (e.g., shift work)
• Work demands—size of workload, intensity, uncertainty, repetitiveness
• Work roles—role conflict, role ambiguity, autonomy, control, job rotation, and job enrichment
• Organizational structure and climate—evaluation and reward systems, turnover, job security, norms, perceived justice, breaches of psychological contracts
• Leadership
• Work-life balance
• Person-organization fit
	• Psychological health
	  – Stress
	  – Depression
	  – Burnout
	• Physical health
	  – High blood pressure
	  – Weight gain
	  – Migraines
	  – Anxiety
	  – Trouble sleeping, exhaustion
	  – Body function or disease
	  – Illness (e.g., catching the flu)
		• Productivity, quality of work
		• Mistakes, accidents, injuries
		• Absenteeism, turnover
		• Counterproductive work behaviors (e.g., stealing office supplies, defacing company property, badmouthing the organization, sabotage)
		• Reduced prosocial activities (e.g., helping coworkers, volunteering to stay late to get work done)
		• Increased health care and disability costs
		• Substance use on the job

Environmental Characteristics	*Attitudes and Perceptions*	*Personal Consequences*

• Situational pressures—weather, commute
• Economic and industry pressures—unemployment, unions, increased training and education requirements for members of certain professions
• Geographic location features—quality of life; cost of living; climate; hours of daylight and sunlight exposure; community's alignment with personal interests, goals, and lifestyle preferences
	• Job satisfaction
	• Family and life happiness
	• Perceived justice, psychological contracts
	• Organizational commitment
		• Individual
		  – Long-term health issues—heart disease, depression, suicide, alcohol and substance abuse, driving accidents
		  – Illegal activity—DUIs, arrests, incarceration
		  – Emotional and financial hardship
		• Family
		  – Unhappiness, fighting, divorce
		  – Abuse
		  – Emotional and financial hardship for the family

Personal Characteristics		
• Demographics—age, gender, race, or ethnicity • Personality and temperament—locus of control, negative affect, emotional stability • Family demands and other life constraints or pressures—work-family conflict, child care needs, financial stability		

SOURCE: Adapted from Hardison et al., 2017, p. 67.

As shown in the center column of the table, several aspects of *well-being* and *attitudes and perceptions* are relevant in the workplace, and they take center stage in many stress-related workplace concerns. These factors can be costly for both employees and employers, resulting in behavioral, physical, and psychological problems. Burnout and depression are potential outcomes of adverse workplace and environmental factors. Employee perceptions regarding the fairness of organizational policies and practices, the ability to balance work and family demands, and job satisfaction can all have negative consequences for individuals and organizations.

As shown in the far-right column of the table, the consequences of poor employee well-being and negative workplace attitudes are far-reaching for employers and employees alike. The *organizational consequences* can include higher rates of absenteeism and turnover, lower productivity and work quality, increased mistakes and accidents, intentional harm to the organization or individuals in the workplace, and higher health expenditures. The spillover effects on personal lives can also be significant. These *personal consequences* affect the health and well-being not only of employees but also of their families.

Taken together, the consequences for organizations are significant. Recruiting and retention alone are not the only reasons that an organization should be concerned about stress and well-being of its employees. Moreover, the landscape of stressors and consequences is complex, and solutions to address them need to account for this complexity. Thus, it is critical that organizations diagnose which issues are relevant in their workforce and for whom as a first step in addressing concerns about a stressed workforce.

Organization of This Report

In the rest of this report, we present the topics that the senior leader stakeholders we interviewed identified as the major sources of stress for National Guard personnel. In Chapter 2, we summarize the types of operations that National Guard personnel have faced since 2020 and leaders' comments about the increased pace of operations as a stressor. In Chapters 3 through 6, we discuss a variety of workforce stressors on National Guard personnel: personnel fundamentals, such as recruiting and retention (Chapter 3); ancillary training and other work demands (Chapter 4); social and lifestyle considerations (Chapter 5); and health care and child care considerations (Chapter 6). In Chapter 7, we conclude with insights from our research and next steps for future research.

CHAPTER 2

Overview of National Guard Operations and Recent Demands

Across federal, state, domestic, and international areas, the National Guard has reached an ongoing level of activity that likely signifies a new, heightened degree of intensity. There is a widespread perception among the Guard's senior leadership that the National Guard has moved into uncharted territory in terms of the level of operational demands being placed on its service members. This pace of operations was described by leaders as one of the central sources of stress on National Guard members and their families.

National Guard Mission Areas

The National Guard conducts operational missions under the following three main mission areas:

1. Federal operations under Title 10[1]
2. Federal operations under Title 32[2]
3. State active duty.

Operations under Title 10 authorities within the U.S. Code involve activations in the Guard's role as a component of the U.S. Army and the U.S. Air Force. Guard personnel fall under the control of active-component units within the services that conduct operations across a range of mission sets. The Guard also conducts federal operations under several authorities included in Title 32 of the U.S. Code, which pertain to operations in defense support to civilian authorities. Under this authority, the Guard provides support for large-scale, prominent events, such as presidential inaugurations, the response to the January 6th attack on the U.S. Capitol, and other designated National Security Special Events.[3] Members of the

---

[1] U.S. Code, Title 10, Armed Forces.

[2] U.S. Code, Title 32, National Guard.

[3] The U.S. Secret Service leads the events after designation from the Department of Homeland Security because the events frequently involve protection of the President of the United States. When oper-

Guard in Title 32 status receive federal pay and benefits while operating under the state's control. As part of its role as a fundamentally dual-missioned force, service members in the National Guard also can be called up by the states. Activations under this category are known as state *active-duty missions* (Kapp, 2023). Under state active duty, service members receive state benefits, pay, and protections.

High Tempo for National Guard Personnel

The leaders that we interviewed highlighted the importance of looking across all the Guard's main mission areas to gain a combined picture of its activity level. Interviewees expressed that the National Guard has maintained a consistently high—albeit varying—level of activity across these mission areas, and there is no sense that the demand for the Guard's capabilities will lessen in the near future. Leaders described this as resulting in both a *high personnel tempo* (PERSTEMPO) and a *high operational tempo* (OPTEMPO). The Congressional Research Service defines these terms as follows:

> PERSTEMPO[—]The amount of time *servicemembers* are engaged in their official duties at a location or under circumstances that make it infeasible for a member to spend off-duty time in the housing in which the member resides.

> OPTEMPO[—]The rate at which *units* are involved in all military activities, including contingency operations, exercises, and training deployments (Kamarck, 2022, p. 1).

Leadership emphasized that the impacts of PERSTEMPO were the most relevant major stressor for individuals. This increased PERSTEMPO, which resulted partly from the increasingly high OPTEMPO since 2020, concerned leaders the most. The Congressional Research Service also noted that high PERSTEMPO is something that DoD should be concerned about:

> In general, research has found associations between deployment frequency and duration, and decreased military spouse well-being (e.g., depression and anxiety), increased child problematic behaviors, and negative effects on parent-child and member-spouse relationships. On the other hand, while many members express dissatisfaction with increased deployments, the evidence does not suggest that has a significant effect on continuation/retention rates. There is some evidence that deployments increase military family savings, potentially reflecting their eligibility for additional compensation (Kamarck, 2022, p. 2).

---

ating under the Title 32 status, the Guard serves under a dual-status commander who also commands active-component and reserve forces operating under Title 10 authorities. The combined military forces in the defense support to civilian authorities' missions are a component of a larger federal, state, and local response. See U.S. Secret Service, undated.

Contemporary National Guard Duties

The National Guard and other reserve components, such as the U.S. Army Reserve or the U.S. Navy Reserve, have transitioned from a strategic reserve, which is ready to supplement the active component during large-scale conflict, to an operational reserve, which is integrated into ongoing missions among a number of areas. In the nation's response to the terrorist attacks of September 11th, 2001, and ensuing operations in Iraq and Afghanistan, more than one million reserve members, including tens of thousands of Guard members, were called to active duty (Kapp and Torreon, 2021).

At the federal level, while Title 10 operations have decreased with the Afghanistan drawdown, activations and deployments continue in support of the National Defense Strategy and the response to the Russian invasion of Ukraine, which began in 2022. In January 2023, approximately 40,000 Guard members were on Title 10 active duty, and more than 22,000 were located abroad. This number is lower than the deployments during the wars in Iraq and Afghanistan and in the Global War on Terrorism, as well as during the significant effort to support the nation's response to the COVID-19 pandemic (Hokanson and Whitehead, 2023). In June 2022, NGB Chief Daniel R. Hokanson testified before the Senate Appropriations Committee that, on average, more than 19,000 Guard members were supporting combat command mission abroad each day (Hokanson, 2022). In 2021, 92,278 National Guard members conducted missions at home or abroad, and 57,601 National Guard members were engaged in 2020. Our interviews also attest to the extensiveness of the Guard's Title 10 mission. For example, one leader explained,

> On the ground side that demand signal is lessened not going to Iraq and Afghanistan, but we do have them in Jordan or Kuwait. There have been emerging missions in Africa. The Air Guard is just as busy, busy as I have ever seen them. They are still rotating in and out of the Middle East.

As for the National Guard's domestic operations, in 2020, the Guard provided more than 7.6 million days in support of the nation's COVID-19 response, along with more than 620,000 days supporting civil authorities in the wake of demonstrations in response to the killing of George Floyd in 2020.[4] At 798,042 days, the southwest border mission, which started in 2006, is among the top draws for operations within the country itself. Other 2020 missions included wildfires (155,000 personnel days), hurricanes (10,600 personnel days), earthquakes (36,700 personnel days), and elections (15,900 days). In 2021, activity levels were similar in COVID-19 response (7.6 million days), wildfire (172,000), weather (220,500), and civil disturbance (Hokanson, 2021).

In 2021, the Guard served more than 10.2 million personnel days conducting domestic operations, whether in a federal Title 32 status or state active duty. More than 29,000 mem-

---

[4] Each of these days is the equivalent of a single Guard member carrying out a mission through one day.

bers of the National Guard were conducting domestic operations on an average day. The National Guard response to the January 6th attack on the U.S. Capitol and its securing of the Presidential Inauguration illustrate the scale of events when the Guard operates in a Title 32 status. That operation involved more than 26,000 Guard members from all states, territories, and the District of Columbia (Hokanson, 2022).

The National Guard leaders interviewed for this study shared that natural disaster response missions—such as wildfires and hurricanes—are growing in scale and intensity.[5] National Guard leaders also expressed the view that National Guard support at the state level outside of natural disaster response is similarly growing and changing in character. The National Guard's capabilities are being tapped to assist and fill in gaps where local and state capabilities are limited in a far more substantial and prominent way than in the past.

The National Guard is being called to state active duty in some states to carry out missions that were previously seen as the responsibility of the federal government. Since 2021, Texas has ordered more than 1,000 service members to active duty to assist in securing the country's border with Mexico to stem migrant flows (Texas Military Department, undated). This operation has occurred over a duration and physical distance typically associated with a large-scale operation abroad, which has led to a variety of stresses on Guard members and families that are similar to those of overseas deployment.

Governors are activating the Guard on state active duty to support state departments and services struggling to meet demands. The COVID-19 pandemic led to unconventional operations under state active duty, including deploying Guard members as substitute teachers, bus drivers, space disinfection teams, and hospital staffing. Members of the Florida and West Virginia National Guard have helped fill staffing shortfalls in the respective states' departments of corrections (Florida Department of Corrections, 2022; West Virginia National Guard, 2022). The National Guard also has been increasingly called to supplement local law enforcement. When the Guard operates under the control of a governor either under Title 32 or state active duty, posse comitatus restrictions against using the National Guard for law enforcement (which would prevent the National Guard from operating side-by-side with local police departments or state law enforcement agencies and with similar authorities, including the ability to make arrests)[6] do not apply.[7]

---

[5] They noted that wildfires and hurricanes have increased in frequency and scale in part because the seasons for these events are lasting longer, the extent of areas that are seeing these events is bigger, and the storms that occur are seemingly more intense and therefore more destructive. They also noted that because of the population density changes that have occurred, the devastation that can result and the population that can be affected are bigger as well.

[6] See Elsea, 2018.

[7] The Posse Comitatus Act restricts the military's direct participation in domestic law enforcement, except in cases when Congress authorizes that involvement (U.S. Code, Title 18, Section 1385, Use of Army and Air Force as Posse Comitatus). The Insurrection Act is one such exception that Congress has authorized (U.S. Code, Title 10, Sections 251–255, Insurrection).

Interviewees identified numerous ways that the changing scale and character of National Guard operations are stressing the force. Governors can task National Guard members to conduct missions outside the core competencies for which the force is organized, trained, and equipped. In the case of law enforcement actions, members of the National Guard can be pitted against members of the communities that they joined the Guard to support. One leader explained that natural disasters, which are largely unavoidable, are sometimes viewed as less stressful and disheartening than the civil conflicts that have also led to state active-duty assignments:

> [It is] the nature of what you are being asked to do. It is easy to get assembled when there is a natural disaster, but [it is harder] when it is man versus man and a domestic response trying to support law enforcement and right to protest and the nefarious element and spiraling to violence. In my generation this isn't something we grew up with. It is really stressful on the team.

However, several interviewees believed that the Guard's involvement in law enforcement operations related to civil demonstrations or disturbances could reveal the Guard's strength as a community-based force. One interviewee referenced the Guard's activities in response to the protests in the wake of the killing of George Floyd. "We said, no verbal, no non-verbal taking sides," mentioned one leader, "We are nonpolitical."

The National Guard and DoD writ large need to be able to monitor and track activities of National Guard members and the character of those activities. Interviewees said they are given updates, but that the information provided by states is often inconsistent. Also, the states do not identify the particular service member who is activated. One senior-level interviewee stated that, during domestic operations, "Our PERSTEMPO is not well-tracked." "The [information] is only as good as the states want us to see," explained another senior leader. "On a good day, we are seeing everything the states are doing but . . . we don't have full visibility." Policy and political difference between the current administration of the federal government and the states can be a barrier to providing the NGB more information:

> Political issues prevent some states from being willing to disclose information (e.g., about stressors, manning, PERSTEMPO, mission demands, etc.). From an NGB guard perspective, without having visibility into that, we can't come up with solutions.

Interviewees expressed concerns that these stressors would become more pronounced as state authorities increasingly look to Guard assistance because of shortfalls in other areas of governmental administration. The common sentiment among those interviewed was that these pop-up support requests will continue for a variety of reasons.

The Stresses of Family Separations and Duty Status Switches

The leaders that we interviewed mentioned that—whether a federal or state mission—Guard deployments often come with a stressful separation from home, families, and professions. Responding to emergencies that are being experienced by the communities in which Guard members and their families live can increase the stress of domestic operations.

Interviewees consistently pointed to stresses that come from activating Guard members under a variety of different federal duty statuses. Pay and benefits vary according to whether a Guard member's service is under Title 10 or Title 32 and whether they are activated for 30 days or longer. According to the interviewees, there are numerous instances in which Guard members serve side by side with other Guard members operating under a different status; active component members on Title 10 receive greater pay and benefits while carrying out the same function. Guard members view all this service as "answering the call to duty," but differences that come from nuances in statute, regulation, or directives create a sense of inequity and lack of support.

Another challenge of operating under a variety of different duty statuses is that members can experience disruption of pay and benefits as they transition on and off active duty. These issues create immediate impacts on family finances and the service members' beliefs that they are being supported to carry out their responsibilities. As one interviewee said,

> With the Guard, we go into and out of many statuses, and COVID really brought that on. Both airmen and army are trying to go to a better pays system. Going between active and guard, [one issue is] the pay system. The worst thing you can do to someone is not pay them on time. That is the worse stressor. You have to [fix the issue of] going in and out of statuses to address that stressor.

Though not the central focus of this study, senior leaders highlighted additional drawbacks of operations under multiple duty statuses, including budgeting and planning. The complications of switching among duty statuses has its most negative effect on the health care available to Guard members and families, which will be discussed in Chapter 6.

The NGB has taken its own steps to mitigate the challenge of personnel activations among multiple duty statuses, including suggesting ways to reduce the number of statuses under which it operates to eight.[8] Congress directed DoD to develop a detailed legislative proposal to consolidate duty statuses.[9] Our interviewees discussed the legislative proposal that would consolidate the 32 statuses down to four categories, which is currently under consideration by the Office of Management and Budget.

---

[8] Note that until the existing proposed legislation on duty status reform becomes law, the NGB cannot reduce its statuses.

[9] The National Defense Authorization Act for Fiscal Year 2018 requires DoD to consolidate Guard and reserve duty statuses (U.S. House of Representatives, National Defense Authorization Act for Fiscal Year 2018, Report 115–404, November 9, 2017).

Unpredictability and Constant Change in Operational Demands

Some comments focused on the unpredictability in the pace of operations. As mentioned previously, leaders noted that there continues to be a steady and predictable demand for Title 10 deployments. One interviewee noted, "Short of a fight tonight, there will be steady demand. That is predictable." However, as explained in Chapter 2, demands encompass both state and federal operations, which leads to a constant need for adaptation and flexibility among Guard members. Leaders talked about how it is largely the state operations that bring a high level of unpredictability. As one explained, "Mostly state [duty] is unpredictable. There are 5,000 guardsmen on active duty at the border," a level that few SMEs would have forecasted five years ago.

One leader explained that balancing the "what if" scenarios for federal operations can be crucial, especially when considering the potential for immediate combat readiness or responding to natural disasters:

> Balancing the what if scenarios for Title 10 [and] the what if we fight tonight, for Title 10
> . . . is a delicate balance. If there is a hurricane, it is all hands on deck. The faster we recover
> from those activities, the [better].

Leaders explained how hard it is to balance demands when unexpected events occur repeatedly and simultaneously. The more events that occur at once, the more the balancing act is undermined, which increases the stress of the force.

National Guard leaders discussed the increasing frequency and expanding geographical scope of environmental events, such as fire seasons and hurricanes, which add to unpredictability. As some leaders noted, these unpredictable demands have always existed, but they seem to be more frequent, for longer periods, and over a wider swath of the country. They noted that the continuous need for assistance is predictable, but that uncertainty lies in determining where and when these events will occur. As one leader commented, it "used to be just a few states."

Leaders talked about how this unpredictability places significant pressure on Guard members as they strive to maintain readiness, respond quickly, and recover from these demanding activities. Effectively managing and recovering from such events becomes essential not only for the mission but also to minimize other potential negative impacts (e.g., on how the public views the guard's resiliency and responsiveness or on recruiting and retention).

CHAPTER 3

Personnel Fundamentals

The Guard's ability to fill its ranks with trained and ready personnel can be both a cause and consequence of the stress on Guard members. Shortages of trained, ready, and available forces require members to carry out additional tasks. As a result, the ability to undertake any activity that is not central to the unit's functioning might be hindered, as well as a member's ability to take leave or move to a less-pressured area. Carrying extra burdens and the sheer lack of recovery time places additional burdens on service members. At the same time, stressors can lead service members to seek transfer out of undermanned units or depart from service altogether, whether through separation or retirement. As word spreads outside of a unit and the larger organization, *recruiting*—engaging candidates to join the service—can be negatively affected.

Stress and these personnel fundamentals (such as retention, recruiting, and manpower availability and fill rates), interact back and forth, creating a potential downward spiral with consequences that can ripple across an organization. Addressing root cause problems can be particularly challenging because of a chicken-or-the-egg dynamic as to which, stressors or staffing shortfalls, causes which. As discussed later in this report, stress can result from a variety of different issues apart from staffing.[1]

Despite senior leader perceptions that the recent PERSTEMPO has been stressful to the force, some leaders noted that the Guard remains healthy in terms of its retention and overall numbers of personnel. Some also noted that retention is a lagging indicator of problems; therefore, we may see a retention problem emerge at some point in the future. In addition, they acknowledged that recruiting continues to be a significant challenge, which mirrors the issues faced by the armed services. Leaders are also concerned about having sufficient personnel to meet full-time staffing requirements and whether the allocation of positions among the states is adequate to meet the demands.

Recruiting

The Army National Guard fell short of its fiscal year 2022 goal by approximately 9,000 members. In addition, Air National Guard Director Lt. Gen. Michael A. Loh announced that the

---

[1] For more discussion of the interaction between these issues, see Hardison et al., 2014.

Air Guard would similarly miss its fiscal year 2023 goal by almost 4,000 recruits (Ware, 2023). Similarly, Army National Guard recruiting challenges were the focus of a recent article (Beynon, 2022).

Some states, which are responsible for their own recruiting, are doing much better than others and have met their recruiting goals. One senior leader we interviewed stated, "I would have guessed we would have fallen off [from our recruiting targets (i.e., lower recruiting numbers)], but we were great."

Senior leaders interviewed for this study ascribe the Guard's challenges to the same factors affecting the active components of the armed services: a lower propensity to serve among eligible recruits and a shrinking pool of eligible recruits because of a lack of physical fitness, low aptitude, or misconduct history. Keying in on the physical fitness of potential candidates, one interviewee said, "Some [potential recruits] cannot make it through MEPS [Military Entrance Processing Station]. . . . The health of our recruits is not as strong as it has been. It hurts our numbers."

Some interviewees added that the attitudes, expectations, and desires of the country's youth population are changing, and the National Guard, along with the rest of the military, has not kept pace. "A lot of [young people] want to grow a beard or color their nails," noted one leader. "Most of our social norms have evolved and they want their personal styles." The perception among the Guard leaders we interviewed is that new potential recruits are deterred by fear of getting injured in the line of duty, a fear that is fed—in their view—by media images and stereotypes of homeless veterans. Concerns over sexual assault and harassment and the broader challenges the military faces in communicating its efforts to resolve those problems might also have a negative effect on recruits. Similarly, in this context, recruits' friends and family who otherwise might encourage them to join—known as *influencers*—might be less likely to do so. Several interviewees cited "woke" culture as a recruiting deterrent, pointing to the COVID-19 vaccine mandate for service members and concerns over diversity, equity, and inclusion initiatives and programs. Lastly, leaders we interviewed said that inspirational ideas, such as answering the call to duty and defending your country, are still seen as motivators to join, but the desire for concrete rewards at minimal cost of service has become noticeable. "People want the benefits," noted one leader, "but there is still a stress about deploying."[2]

---

[2] Note that some caution is warranted in interpreting the ideas offered by leaders with respect to recruiting deterrents. Views of propense youth about why they are or are not willing to serve in the National Guard may differ notably from those expressed in our interviews by leadership. To determine whether leadership's ideas about these types of recruiting deterrents are correct, we recommend that the NGB further explore whether existing research by the DoD's Joint Advertising Market Research & Studies program addresses the specific topics raised by leaders here (e.g., "woke" culture, COVID-19 mandates, etc.) and their impacts on willingness to serve. If such topics have not been explored by the Joint Advertising Market Research & Studies program, we suggest that studies be designed to explore them.

Retention

According to the leaders that we interviewed, despite the increased PERSTEMPO, retention still appears strong. They said that a high pace of activity contributes to retention because Guard members are carrying out the mission that might have drawn them to join in the first place. "The more busy we have gotten," said one leader, "the more we have retained people. They are doing great." The general sentiment among those interviewed for this report is that high OPTEMPO encourages Guard members to stay rather than leave the force. Guard members desire and expect to be busy with training and deployments.

However, interviewees also expressed the belief that Guard members decide to leave under particularly high OPTEMPO, especially when activations come right after another. The issue is "the overall ops tempo," said an interviewee. "It's being gone for a year and then getting hit up stateside." Such comments raise the issue of whether there is a turning point at which operations that draw a Guard member to serve simply become too much to sustain. Such a tipping or turning point is worth further exploration. In June 2023, the Army Guard was 63 percent of the way toward its retention goal of 37,000 personnel, and recent reporting suggests that there might be looming retention challenges (Beynon, 2023).

Moreover, there is a perception that members of the Guard are joining to achieve specific ends, perhaps to gain a particular skill, credential, or benefit. Members are staying in service for "six years and then they punch out after the education benefit," said one senior leader during an interview. "We used to say, 'What's six more years?!' That is not how it is today." National Guard leaders also believe that life decisions are driving longtime service members to leave, perhaps the difficulty of balancing the responsibilities of service with the demands of caring for a family. "Stressors are causing people to leave," said one interviewee. "I am going to take on a supervisory role, and I am going to become a commander, and have a baby." In the view of several interviewees, Guard members are having children later in life, coinciding with the point in a Guard member's career that they take on greater supervisory responsibility and time commitments. "It used to be if you got in, you said you were good to go for 20 years, but then they [stayed for] 28," explained one interviewee. "Now, they are leaving at 20. You used to have to throw them out!" These issues, along with perceived excessive training demands, will be explored in later chapters.

Manpower Requirements, Fill-Rates, and Difficulties Staffing the Force

Shortfalls in recruiting and shorter careers make it more difficult to fill units with trained and ready personnel. That said, our interviewees view the Guard as being able to balance among its units and maintain them at a sufficient strength.

However, assuming that the demands of domestic operations continue, some interviewees suggested that personnel authorizations among the states need to be rebalanced. Leaders cited differences in the number of members of the Guard per capita across the states and a misalignment between where Guard forces are located and where the nation's population lives as reasons why rebalancing needs to be examined. Similarly, Guard leaders expressed the strong desire to continue to increase full-time staffing within units. These full-time personnel, who usually serve under an Active Guard Reserve status, provide daily continuity within units and are critical for unit readiness and for supporting unit members. The interviewees acknowledged the critical role that services play in setting manpower allocations based on military requirements.

CHAPTER 4

Administrative Work Demands

When asked about the stressors the workforce faces, leaders discussed several topics that compound PERSTEMPO stressors. In this chapter, we cover the topics related to training demands and other types of administrative burdens, including a discussion of how ancillary training demands and the difficulties in accessing that training can add to stress. We also include comments related to the added stress and burden of organizational and bureaucratic hurdles. Leaders commented about how uncertainty and unpredictability in work demands are stressors, and certain types of assignments or missions are more stressful than others. Lastly, they discussed the difficulty in funding and resourcing programs as another source of stress for staff.

Ancillary Training Burdens

Leaders commented that training can add to the stress and burdens of the workforce. For example, there is an expectation that Guard members will complete some of the ancillary training on their own time, in addition to their full-time jobs and one-weekend-a-month National Guard commitment. As one leader explained, "We put on airmen a lot [of training] to do on their own time—that is a stressor."

Leaders' comments about training demands were not all negative, however. Some also talked about how training has gotten better over the years, partly because of computer and online delivery, which allows for more distance learning, self-paced training, and virtual learning. They explained that this increased online and virtual access to training can be good because it allows people to complete training whenever they have the time available. It also means that more training can be completed remotely instead of requiring a commute to a drilling station or other location.

Although automated training was generally viewed as a positive, one leader pointed out that it takes time for new training to become automated. If training is constantly changing, automation that introduces more flexibility into the training might not be practical. As a result, many training programs that are considered burdensome might not be helped by automation. As one leader said, "[we are] constantly getting new programs and sometimes it exceeds the automation capability."

Additionally, one leader noted that if the technology works, it is generally viewed as a positive. However, there are many obstacles to technology working smoothly, such as technical glitches, issues with computer access, or inadequate Wi-Fi access.

One leader also talked about the delicate balance between training readiness and unit readiness, particularly in the context of the COVID-19 pandemic. When asked about the impact of the pandemic on readiness, interviewees said it might have been beneficial in some ways but detrimental in others. In their view, the pandemic increased short-term readiness in some cases by allowing some people to apply their skills in a real-world setting (e.g., medical personnel supporting the COVID-19 response), but it also may have resulted in a loss of unit integrity in the long term.

Similarly, other interviewees were also concerned about the impact of high OPTEMPO on the ability to participate in training to maintain skills for Title 10 missions. Participants noted that, with limited time and increased responsibilities resulting from the higher OPTEMPO, there was a smaller margin for error, which makes deteriorating skills an even bigger concern. This sentiment highlighted the pressure individuals felt to maintain their proficiency while managing other duties. To elaborate on this, leaders noted that many of the domestic missions have required personnel to be employed in ways that they historically have not been employed (driving buses; working in schools, hospitals, and prisons; deploying to the border, etc.). Because of these atypical uses of personnel, leaders are concerned that personnel do not have enough practical experience relevant to their usual profession and that they are not allowed enough time to maintain their core training in their field. As a result, their readiness for a mission that would tap their core specialty might be degraded.

Bureaucracy Causing More Work

Leaders we interviewed raised a variety of concerns about the impacts of bureaucratic administrative procedures and procedural hurdles on stress. They talked about how there are many documentation requirements and form-filling tasks that are viewed as unnecessarily time-consuming, frustrating, and mentally draining. They explained how simply completing paperwork is just one more thing that takes their time away from families and the mission.

Leaders explained that systems often do not talk to each other and therefore require manual reentry from one system to the next. They also talked about how these bureaucratic systems lead to unnecessary delays because of multiple layers of decisionmaking, lengthy approval processes, and even paperwork falling through the cracks.

Leaders offered multiple concrete examples of bureaucratic frustrations. For example, one commented that "senior staff are having everything reviewed by legal," which adds another layer to the bureaucratic process. They also mentioned the time it takes to get "policies, telework, or COVID shots" as an example of the variety of processes that people find frustrating. Some gave examples of second-order problems that result from the bureaucratic delays and are stressful for the workforce. For example, one leader talked about how stressful it is when members are not paid in a timely manner: "We have antiquated systems for our pay. We are changing our statuses and then the pay systems don't catch up…we [end up not paying] them for like six weeks." Leaders talked about how this is especially stressful for service members who have child care bills, rent, and other financial obligations that are due and are counting on their pay coming through. They also talked about how this stresses leaders who see this happening to their service members and are unable to fix it.

Lastly, one noted that bureaucratic processes are a problem not only for those who are interacting with the system but also for those who manage the systems: One leader gave the following example of someone describing the programs they manage to a senior leader:

> She had listed every program that she was responsible for and said, "this one takes like six hours." He gets to the medical one and . . . he says "wow, you spend all of your time just managing the systems."

Unpredictability and Uncertainty Not Related to Operations

Although much of the discussion about unpredictability focused on operations, leaders also noted that unpredictability can come about in other ways, as well. For example, one leader talked about the "constant churn of people on staffs" and how the uncertainty regarding who will be on the staff, the loss of expertise, and the need to continually train new people who will soon turn over again adds to stress. The need to uproot someone's family for a new assignment is also stressful. In addition, one mentioned the "stress [resulting from] unpredictability of last-minute decisions," explaining that permanent change of station decisions or renewal of someone's assignment are often made at the 11th hour. This puts stress on the service members and their families who are waiting to find out if they will be staying in their assignment or leaving.

Insufficient Funding

A few leaders raised funding as a stressor in our interviews. They talked generally about not having enough funding to cover a needed person or not having the funding to support a program. They also talked about how, in certain cases, a lack of funding sends a signal that people are not valued.

A few leaders raised the idea that funding was one of the many obstacles to instituting programs and technologies that might help reduce stressors overall. For example, leaders commented that there is not enough funding to provide personnel with laptops or iPads, which could increase access to online training, distance learning, or remote work, as well as a feeling of connectedness. Some leaders noted that funding was potentially an obstacle for creating broader access to relevant programs (e.g., the pilot child care program) and health care coverage, both discussed in subsequent chapters. However, one leader posited that funding was probably not the real issue; instead, the real obstacle was ensuring that personnel are aware of and have access to all the programs that already exist.

CHAPTER 5

Social and Lifestyle Considerations

Leaders also mentioned social and lifestyle considerations as stressors among National Guard personnel. This included a general sense that personnel were less interpersonally connected to each other than they were in the past. Interviewees also expressed the belief that people were living and working in more dispersed locations across the state that were farther from their home drilling stations than people had been in the past. In addition, more Guard personnel want to work remotely since the return to work after the COVID-19 pandemic.

Lack of Interpersonal Connectedness

Some leaders highlighted the greater degree of disconnectedness among the workforce than in the past, driven perhaps by the longer distances people travel to drill or for their assignments:

> We don't get the touch points. It is the two days a month, we used to be a family force, you knew everybody. If I could go back to that I would. All of those things were wrapped up in that community. Now we are more like the active component. We have people driving past each other to go to drill. We are better trained and equipped. But before we could take care of our own because we knew who was hurting and what they needed. Now we only have two days a month.

> We don't see each other outside of work much. Everyone gets on the metro and goes home. When it is needed, we are here but generally we are living an hour away. . . . They are definitely living further.

Another reason that was mentioned was the move to teleworking as a result of COVID-19.

One participant pointed out that disconnectedness might be partly a consequence of intentional personnel management decisions to move people around for career broadening experiences. They explained that those decisions might be beneficial to personnel in other ways:

> This is a big change from how the Guard used to be. . . . Their father was there and their grandfather was there and their kids will be. That was how it used to be. It was too stovepiped, and we have been encouraging spreading people out and to get the perspective, but . . . the downside is that people are more disconnected. If they are in one place, they are old style, but we are trying to broaden them now.

Another leader talked about how the level of disconnectedness and reasons for it might differ depending on the state in which personnel live:

> I think there are 54 different conversations. There are some states that are struggling the most with the discussion I just said [disconnectedness]. You will find pockets where grandfathers and brothers have all served and I would argue that you have less stress in those pockets.

Yet another leader talked about how connectedness can differ by service because of the structure and frequency of assignments and how personnel are utilized:

> Air Guard is more connected because they join a wing and stay in it. The Army had a law on the books that said you would have a unit in every community. But then we cut costs, so Air Guard is more connected. They are more centrally located so they have more access to things to reduce stressors. Now, the use factor is still a contributor for the air side. There is still a high demand for Title 10. When I joined, it was a community. Today we are consolidated, moving around, moving for career opportunities. A 35-year-old colonel will have a different perspective.

One consequence of the lack of connection that was discussed was that leaders and supervisors have less visibility into problems that individuals might be having. For example, this topic was talked about at length in relation to suicides.

Interviewees mentioned a few ideas that might help increase connectedness and remedy the negative consequences. For example, one participant talked about the potential benefits of providing everyone with a laptop or an iPad and ensuring they all had adequate Wi-Fi access:

> [The concern is about the] population between 18 to 24. If I had all the resources in the world, everyone one would have an iPad and be connected. They are into texting. [We say things like] 'we can't afford all of the licensees so every E4 is not allowed.' If the E4 has a phone [then people] can communicate that they are having a problem with their E4. . . . It is important to leaders on the ground.

Leaders mentioned reducing teleworking as a potential solution, but they also noted that people are asking for more teleworking opportunities, illustrating the notable complexities in addressing the lack of connection. Another leader debated the pros and cons of a decision to do as much as possible electronically so that time spent together could be as valuable as possible. On the one hand, interviewees noted that doing more online was possible only in certain types of missions. On the other hand, they noted that doing more online made it easier to find time when everyone was available to meet in person, allowing face-to-face time to be used more wisely. They explained,

> [we] did see that it was easier to coalesce them if you could augment what you could get done electronically. The mission really drove how you were doing that mission set. But

what that does is that you have changed the paradigm. An interesting thing that I wonder [is,] what did we improve and at what expense?

Distance and Its Impacts on Access to Services and Commute Times

Although distance is related to interconnectedness, the impacts of distance and living in remote locations on people's access to services and their commute times can be a stressor in and of itself. One interviewee commented,

> [In my location] I can go get lawyers, mental health, and finance help. In the 54 [States, Territories, and the District of Columbia, there are many locations where] you don't have access. You need financial help, and there is only one guy in the whole state.

With respect to commute times, a few of the leaders talked about people traveling far for work, assignments, or drilling and how that long commute itself could be a potential added stressor or burden for those individuals. One participant stated that some states might have metrics to examine the distance and how it has changed over time. Leaders also said that the issue of commute distance is a bigger problem for certain states:

> The states look at data on how far people live from their unit and how that has changed over time. . . . [In one state] the average drive was [around 160] miles, even if an armory was 20 miles away, they didn't belong to that unit.

Return to Work After COVID-19

A few leaders noted that it was difficult to get some people to come back to work after the COVID-19 pandemic. They noted that some people really want to work remotely (or do as much of their training and administrative activities as they can remotely) and are frustrated by the lack of remote work options. The pressure to return to in-person work was viewed as a stressor for some—particularly when it meant long commute times, finding child care, and a lack of flexibility of work hours. Leaders were concerned that for those people who want to continue to work remotely, the stress of the return to work might lead them to look for work elsewhere.

At the same time, leaders noted that not everyone likes remote work. Some people found the isolation of remote work during the pandemic to be stressful. Additionally, leaders also agree that increasing the amount of remote work brings other challenges, including a lack of connectedness and a lack of visibility into personal issues. Lastly, a few leaders noted that some jobs are simply not amenable to remote work.

CHAPTER 6

Health Care Considerations

The topic of health care, including mental health care, was discussed by several leaders at length. It was described as one of the most frustrating stressors because it has potentially devastating impacts on some members and their families. Leaders described several different types of concerns surrounding access to health care and the resulting stress on the force. They also acknowledged that fixing many of these issues would require a significant investment of taxpayer resources.

Gaps in Coverage

Leaders expressed concerns about gaps in health care coverage and talked about how eligibility for coverage changes depending on status (shown in Table 6.1). The Appendix provides a more detailed summary.

TABLE 6.1

Summary of Health Care Options Available to National Guard Members by Status

Status	Service Member Options	Family Member Options
Not activated	• TRS	• TRS • TRICARE Young Adult
Pre-activation/activated	• TRICARE Prime • TRICARE Prime Remote	• TRICARE Prime • TRICARE Prime Remote for Active Duty Family Members • US Family Health Plan (depending on location) • TRICARE Select • TRICARE Young Adult
Deactivated	• TRS • TRICARE Prime (if in a prime service area) and in the Transitional Assistance Management Program) • Continued Health Care Benefit Program	• TRS • TRICARE Prime (if in a prime service area and in the Transitional Assistance Management Program) • TRICARE Young Adult • Continued Health Care Benefit Program

SOURCE: TRICARE, 2022.

NOTE: TRS = TRICARE Reserve Select.

Leaders talked generally about how notably coverage differs across the different statuses. For example, one leader said, "If someone asks do they get health care when they deploy, my answer is yes with a huge asterisk." Another explained:

> On a federal mobilization, TRICARE kicks in 90 days before you deploy. You have health care before and after. Other places the orders kick in early, and in some cases, they are reliant on their own health care.

Leaders explained that many service members can be entirely uncovered at any given time. For example, according to one leader, "We have about 6,000 or more that don't have health care." They also talked about how coverage on state activation, specifically, is lacking, with one saying, for example, "There are times on the state side that you don't have health care" and "On the state side, if you get hurt, they pay but it isn't the same." Leaders also mentioned that lack of coverage sometimes occurs because young people decide not to pay for the coverage that is available.

In addition, administrative hurdles were raised as well. One leader summarized the findings from a recent survey that identified people's top concerns and issues with the health care systems and recalled the way that some of the participants talked about their struggles navigating the systems:

> The dental insurance says I can do this thing, my dentist submitted the paperwork, and it is not accepted, and then it becomes this paperwork back and forth and back and forth. Another category [is] when you are on orders for more than 30 days [and] you are eligible. E.g., you have orders for 90 days and [you] are now eligible, but someone needs to go enter you into another system, and someone looks and says you aren't in the system.

Availability of Providers

Multiple leaders talked about a lack of available providers covered by TRS in the communities where National Guard service members live. They noted that while the strength of the Guard is that its service members are dispersed across a state, this also makes it harder for service members to access care through TRICARE providers. In addition, interviewees noted that it might often look like there are TRICARE service providers near a service member, but those providers might not actually be available. Leaders explained that providers are allowed to restrict their patient community to include only one patient under TRICARE, which limits their availability to the service members.

A few leaders offered analogies to explain their frustration: "It's like if I give you a dollar and say go buy yourself a soda but the vending machine is empty." They also talked about how providers further limit their availability in other ways. For example, one interviewee mentioned that sometimes providers take only cash:

We were sitting in a meeting talking about behavioral health, and they said only 2 percent of the behavioral health providers will take TRICARE and they are doing cash only transactions. What does that mean for a Guard member or family member who is trying to go get mental health care not related to a deployment?

Leaders also talked about impacts of health care issues on retention:

We are looking at it on the benefits side, a premium free solution, thinking "what can we do outside the box?" . . . Trying to make it more attractive for service—if you are down in the 54 [States, Territories, and the District of Columbia,] if you are a dual status and [your spouse] is a traditional Guardsman, [they] can go ahead and get on TRICARE select. There are people who are finding other opportunities.

Administrative Impacts from Changes in Status

Another stressor is associated with the administrative burdens and coverage gaps that occur when duty statuses change. Service members can lose coverage at many points if paperwork is not completed properly, within the appropriate window, by the correct personnel, or is lost because of a clerical error. Leaders talked about how just "navigating the system" can be stressful. For example, the following paperwork requirements under TRICARE (2022, p. 11, emphasis added) exemplifies how coverage gaps can arise:

If you lose coverage under another TRICARE option due to your [spouse's] change in status, you may qualify for TRS or TRR [TRICARE Retired Reserve]. Submit the *Reserve Component Health Coverage Request Form* (DD Form 2896-1) **within 90 days of losing other TRICARE coverage to avoid a break in coverage.** TRS or TRR coverage begins the day after you lose your prior TRICARE coverage.

In addition, leaders talked about continuity of care problems that are particularly problematic for service members and their families who have chronic health care issues or long-term health care needs. Some leaders described situations in which a member or their dependent might be seeing a specialist at the time of a status transition; if that specialist is not covered under the health care provided in the new status, the family will need to find a new provider and move their medical records over to the new provider. That new provider now has no history or rapport with the patient, which can create a major disruption in care. For example, as one leader explained:

They don't understand that they need a different doctor each time . . . [imagine I'm a] college student [and] I'm going to get married, now I will get TRICARE standard. Now to mobilization, now I have to find a provider not only for me but also for my wife . . . . Now take a special care needs child. And you have to deploy, and now I have a civilian employer, do I keep them on my TRICARE or my employer's insurance? This matters.

> We are working on equity . . . Now we are going to deal with a hurricane or civil unrest.
> I could go on state duty and get injured, and that is workman's comp, and now I have an
> injury that renders me undeployable and now I am discharged.

Moreover, ensuring continuous health care coverage is a medical readiness issue, which is critical to operations. As one leader explained:

> You need to be medically ready . . . The issue here is a constant access to health care—not
> an episodic care issue. The nation and the states are relying quite heavily on the National
> Guard for skills to support situations. . . . You are expected to be ready.

In addition, some leaders were concerned about the readiness impacts of personnel postponing care because of gaps in coverage. The example of postponing the treatment of dental issues is just the tip of the iceberg when it comes to service members' deferred medical care:

> We see dental issues; they haven't seen a dentist in five years. They come in before they
> deploy, [and if there are dental issues, it is likely that] there are other issues that they may
> not want to talk about.

One leader noted that Congress is putting funding toward dental readiness, which will certainly help, but leaders also indicated that more still needs be done to improve medical readiness more broadly.

Leaders also talked about the costs to personnel. Some commented about how most of the coverage options are fairly inexpensive for the service members:

> [If y]ou have TRICARE Reserve Select, you have to pay for it. It is not hugely expensive.
> For a single soldier, it's around 60 a month; for a family it's like 250 a month. The active-
> duty folks don't pay for anything. That's gotten better over time.

Lastly, one leader also talked about how people can qualify in multiple statuses at once because of various family member statuses. For example, people can be considered a service member while also being a spouse of a service member (in the case of a dual military household); they can also be a service member's child. The leader described how this adds complexity to the system that the system cannot currently address.

Ideas for New Programs to Address the Health Care Challenges

Leaders offered suggestions for ways to address health care issues. Some suggested that the duty status reform efforts that are underway might help but noted that they will take a long time to implement. Another leader suggested that the Veterans Affairs (VA) health care system could be used to help fill some of the provider gaps:

> TRICARE is challenged to get health care providers because there just aren't enough out there. But definitely [we want to aim for] equity in health care coverage. . . . We had a conversation with the VA about where there could be providers. We know that the vet force is an aging force. There are places that could see Guardsmen with TRICARE. . . . You have this whole VA structure in place, so could we partner more with the VA to get at this?

Some leaders talked about the possibility of making more telemedicine available. This was viewed as having the potential to assist with continuity of care providers for service members who are transitioning across statuses and are far from available providers or specialists. Telemedicine was also discussed with respect to access to mental health care, in particular, and to other types of specialists. In addition, some talked about ways to capitalize on existing military treatment facilities to address the gaps in providers.

Some of the leaders we spoke with generally indicated that the ideal would be one health care solution, regardless of duty status, which is available to everyone and their families for the entirety of their career:

> What would be ideal is, if I come into the military, I have health care coverage and I have a provider of my choice and I can keep that provider through the duration, my kids could keep the same providers, etc. . . . This is a stressor.

> What would I like to see fixed? How can we be more efficient? If I could [do anything regardless of costs], I would want everyone to have health care and a provider that they want. Being a citizen soldier is an amazing thing.

That said, many we spoke with acknowledged that such a change might be financially infeasible. One leader noted how extending coverage to everyone regardless of status, which would be costly, would not solve the entire problem. There would still be a lack of availability of providers unless the government is willing to pay them more to become TRICARE providers. In recognition of what a vast and complex problem this is, one leader explained:

> Thinking outside of the box, how can we create more [access to health care] that can be utilized? . . . If we increase the rate that we pay [TRICARE providers,] that means fewer people can be seen . . . sometimes you can't go a straight line between two points. If you can find a way to reduce the statuses to two or three, or start off with [addressing the issues with people's] teeth, so everyone gets a dental exam, that is a quick win . . . [I]t is a huge problem: Fix one [thing,] it causes another. This is the same problem they are trying to solve in the civilian community.

Although there was a general sense that the costs would be high to fix the entire system the way it truly needs to be fixed, some leaders also acknowledged that small changes or partial changes that might not be as costly could still help.

Mental Health Concerns

Several leaders we interviewed mentioned that mental health issues and access to mental health services are a particular area of concern. Some talked about how it is especially difficult for people who are geographically dispersed to get access to mental health professionals, especially in rural locations. For example:

> I have one director of psychological health centered in the [one] part of the state, and that is a challenge. The wing is similar in the sense that you have people coming to the wing and one director of national health. We don't have [mental health care] billets in the Air National Guard, at least [not] here. And [this is a problem that relates] back to the scarcity of professionals in the less populated areas.

> Those that do have coverage are not around prime service areas. . . . We know that there is a shortage of health care providers, doctors, etc., but the behavioral health is challenging. We had nothing, now we have something.

Leaders also talked about what might be driving some of the mental health issues and stressors. Some talked about mental health issues that result from life in general, beyond a Guard member's work in the military. For example,

> I'm not happy with how our suicide prevention efforts have been. . . . [We have lost more Guardsmen to suicide] than car accidents, or any other thing. We have been doing deep dives on the failures with suicides. It's not about PTSD [posttraumatic stress disorder] or deployments, it's about kids not equipped to handle their emotions and their lives. Most have been in their 20s. Most had a relationship issue, along with some drug use or alcohol use. So those resiliency efforts have to start showing progress. It's so disappointing to me. Separation, divorce, financial [troubles are issues too]. Social isolation from COVID has impacted things. But really an inability to cope with life adult problems.

Others talked about mental health issues tied directly to the work and certain mission sets. For example, one leader said "It could be [the] stress of dealing with a hurricane and knocking on doors and seeing dead people. There are challenges with that." Lastly, one interviewee talked about the importance of making sure that there is a supportive culture in which mental health care needs are not stigmatized, which leads to blind spots where leaders are unaware of issues:

> How do we maintain professional bearing but have a space where we recognize that people are affected by [stress and have resulting mental health issues]? These [issues with stigma] are societal things. . . . Those are stressors in the workforce and if you are not talking about them . . . then they fester.

CHAPTER 7

Child Care Issues

In addition to the extensive discussions about health care, leaders also talked at length about child care as a major source of stress for the subset of the workforce with children. In general, child care stressors can be a significant issue for many working parents. In the military, this issue can be exacerbated by the demands of deployment, which typically take personnel away from their families for extended periods. When a National Guard member is deployed (either for state or federal missions), they might have to leave their children behind and arrange for their care while they are away. Child care is sometimes needed not only during typical daytime workday hours, but also during evenings, weekends, and even overnight.

That said, leaders noted that National Guard personnel face added child care stressors beyond those associated with typical military deployments. Many of the issues raised by leaders were related to a lack of available and affordable child care options for National Guard personnel in particular. Specifically, depending on where a National Guard member is stationed, there may be limited options for affordable and reliable child care, which can add to the stress of trying to balance work and family responsibilities.

Existing Programs

A variety of child care options are available to support National Guard members and their families. The following are some of the available options:[1]

- *Child Development Centers*: These include child care centers that are on base or nearby and provide care for children of military personnel, including National Guard members. These centers typically provide care for children from infancy to age five. They offer *full-day care* (not to exceed ten hours) on a regularly scheduled, daily basis. They also offer *part-day care*, which includes hourly short-term care and the "Give Parents a Break Program," which provides care once a month in the evening or on weekends (My Air Force Benefits, 2023).
- *Family Child Care*: This program offers a network of certified and trained family child care providers who care for children of National Guard members in their homes. Family

---

[1] Some of these options are only available at military installations and only when on active-duty status.

child care offers flexible care options, including full-day, part-time, and before- and after-school care.

- *School Age Care*: This program provides care for school-age children before and after school hours and on school holidays. Care under the program might be located on or off the installation and offer activities, homework assistance, and supervision.

However, eligibility for child care options differs depending on whether a member is drilling, on federal active duty, or on state active duty. For example, members on state active duty are not eligible to use Child Development Centers (My Air Force Benefits, 2023). Army and Air Force sites provide links to various resources for National Guard families to explain their options and connect them with resources and care providers. For example, the My Air Force Benefits website (see My Air Force Benefits, 2022, and My Air Force Benefits, 2023) directs members to the following sites:

- Military Childcare, undated
- ChildCare Aware of America, undated-a.

The National Guard has started a new pilot program to support personnel who are drilling on the weekends. That program, the Army National Guard Weekend Drill Child Care Program, is currently being tested in six states (Massachusetts, New Hampshire, New Mexico, Ohio, Virginia, and Washington) (ChildCare Aware of America, undated-b).

Guard-Specific Child Care Challenges

Although some child care programs and options are available to Guard personnel, leaders have noted that Guard personnel face different challenges accessing those services relative to most Regular Army and Air Force personnel.[2] For example, in our discussions, one leader described the inability to forecast needs and the consequences for securing child care:

> They just don't have an ability to find child care in 48 hours. Even if they can put together something quickly, it isn't long lasting, so it starts to unravel . . . People are willing to do some limited things but it just isn't enough.

The COVID-19 pandemic exacerbated preexisting child care problems. Some leaders mentioned that many day cares closed during the pandemic and some never reopened, suggesting

---

[2] Several of these same child care issues have been described by others. For example, in a 2021 article in *Reserve + National Guard Magazine* (Cunningham, 2021), the author quotes a parent who says she has had to miss drill weekends because she could not find child care and has had to pay for family to travel from far away to help out at times. The author also mentions some of the same concerns about a lack of approved providers in dispersed guard locations.

that there may be even fewer child care options available after the COVID-19 pandemic than before. One leader also talked about the need to stay home with sick children, stating,

> COVID is making this harder . . . so when you have a [care] issue, one of you can't work. Someone has to stay home. This becomes a challenge to recruiting people especially if you have two people who want to serve.

Interviewees also explained that finding care specifically for drill weekends can be especially difficult because providers are not typically open on the weekends, and not for the long hours that might be required (e.g., 12 hours at a time). Since drill weekends occur only once a month and not every week, it is even harder to find consistent care:

> For drill weekend, with the salaries we are paying, we can't find someone who wants to work on the weekend—the providers don't want to work on the weekend. To get a provider to run a certified program on the weekends, we can't pay enough to get them to work for us.

The pilot program targeting care for drill weekends (the Army National Guard Weekend Drill Child Care Program described earlier in this chapter) was mentioned by some of our participants as a potentially promising way to address child care needs. But in addition to the program being available only in some pilot locations, leaders also noted that its limitations might hinder access where it is available. For example, someone must verify that there is no other adult in the home who can care for the children before the service member is considered eligible for the services. This verification requirement adds another administrative paperwork hurdle (which is another added stressor and time burden), and it might slow the system's response to an immediate child care need.

Some leaders also talked about the fact that the dispersion of Guard personnel makes it especially difficult for personnel looking for care to find someone qualified. Personnel near a military base are more likely to be able to find approved care providers simply because there is a market demand for providers. Moreover, unlike Regular Army or Regular Air Force personnel, National Guard personnel who are dispersed across a state do not necessarily have a network of other service members living nearby whom they can lean on for supplemental child care help when needed.

More than one leader expressed concern that the lack of child care access will affect retention. One also noted that personnel with children likely need to leave drilling events as soon as possible to relieve child care providers and might miss out on bonding opportunities after drilling is over, which further exacerbates the disconnectedness concerns mentioned earlier. Finally, one leader mentioned that being flexible in the types of demands that are placed on Guard members could help accommodate these known child care issues and said that to the extent that leaders can be flexible, they should be.

CHAPTER 8

Insights and Next Steps

In this report, we delved into the different stressors facing the National Guard workforce. We presented them across six chapters as relatively discrete issues so that they could be explored in depth. However, many of these stressors are interrelated. For example, changing duty status, which is a defining feature of National Guard operations, is not stressful only because of the changing nature of the work that Guard members perform; it also affects health care coverage for members and their families and generates additional administrative and bureaucratic burdens. Similarly, the pace of operations can affect a member's ability to secure child care. Awareness of the interrelationships among stressors is important when considering solutions. Table 8.1 provides a summary of the full set of issues that leaders raised in their discussions.

Recommended Next Steps for the National Guard

This study was intended as a first look at stressors within the National Guard workforce to gain a broad understanding of the issues that are of greatest concern to leaders. Defining the scope of issues is an important foundational step in making policy recommendations. It helps leaders to see the full array of issues that they likely need to address and consider which of them to prioritize. Identifying and describing sources of stress also helps to illustrate the complexity of these stressors and why making policy changes in one area might not be enough. However, listing the stressors cannot help define the specific policy solutions that are needed in any given area. For that, deep dives into individual topics would be needed, which was beyond the scope of this report.

With this in mind, we recommend that the National Guard conduct targeted research on several key topics that could benefit from additional data collection and exploration to inform and support effective policies.

- **Continue with deeper dives into the topic of workforce stress in the National Guard population.**
  - **Conduct follow-on focus groups and surveys with the broader workforce to explore their views on stressors.** During our interviews, multiple leaders commented that it would be ideal to also ask the same questions of the workforce directly. They

TABLE 8.1

Summary of the Stressors Raised by Leaders

Broad Topic Areas	Specific Issues the SMEs Raised
Nature of National Guard Operations	
Pace of operations	• Increased pace of state-level operations since 2020 (civil unrest, COVID-19, border missions) • Changes in natural disasters (larger areas, longer seasons, increased population impacts) • Lack of visibility into and tracking of state-level PERSTEMPO
Duty status changes	• Disruptions in pay and benefits
Type of demand and morale	• Impact varies across types of assignment (e.g., manmade versus natural), and people differ in their preferences • How governors' use of National Guard can impact morale
Unpredictability and constant change in OPTEMPO	• Unpredictability in the pace of operations leads to stress
Family separations	• People away from family, during COVID-19 in particular • Frustration with some assignments not seeming to be good use of Guard personnel
Personnel Fundamentals	
Recruiting	• Recruiting is a problem, but the issue is not unique to the National Guard
Retention	• Retention does not seem to be a problem so far, yet leaders are concerned about the future • In particular, health care, remote work, child care were noted as possible drivers of retention
Staffing requirements	• Lack of visibility into numbers of personnel needed or utilized at the state level • Some states may be stretched thin whereas others are not
Ancillary Training and Other Work Demands	
Training	• Automation and self-pacing is good • Internet access issues • Atrophying skills
Bureaucracy	• Status changes affect pay and health care (handoffs are not seamless) • Creating more work and detracting from the mission
Unpredictability (not OPTEMPO-related)	• Constant churn of people on staffs • Stress of last-minute decisions
Funding	• Lack of resources to support various needs
Social and Lifestyle Considerations	
Interpersonal connectedness	• Increased disconnectedness often because of remote work and dispersion • Support network missing • Issue visibility is reduced
Distance and remoteness	• Traveling far for drilling • Commute cost and time • Access to services
Return to work after COVID-19	• Some people want remote work • Private-sector remote work might lead people to not join or stay

Table 8.1—Continued

Broad Topic Areas	Specific Issues the SMEs Raised
Health Care Considerations	
Mental health impacts	• Lack of access to mental health providers • Need to normalize seeking mental health care for stress
Health care access issues	• Mental health providers are hard to find • Few doctors serve TRICARE; some accept only a few patients • Access limited in remote locations; VA care was suggested as a supplement
Transition across duty statuses	• Coverage changes by status • Can result in lack of coverage or affect continuity of care • Can create issues for family members • Leads to paperwork burden, delays in coverage
Child Care Considerations	
Weekend care	• Hard to find weekend care, especially since the need is infrequent (once a month) • Heading straight home after drilling to minimize need for care
Transitioning across statuses	• Gaps in care and lags in care options resulting from status changes • Paperwork and administrative hurdles at transition points • State accommodations vary
Cost and remote location options	• Remote location care options are limited • Providers do not view pay as attractive, so there are few options • Difficulty in getting vetted as a provider • Disconnectedness makes it worse • COVID-19 led to day care closures

explained that leadership's views are limited, and relying solely on leadership's understanding of the issues could miss important concerns that the workforce is facing. We recommend a follow-on effort using focus groups and surveys to gather insights and concerns about stressors from the workforce directly. The goal would be to identify the stressor areas of most pressing concern to the workforce (including both those that are most severe and those that are most prevalent) and propose preliminary ways to address or mitigate them. The survey could serve as a baseline effort that could be repeated regularly to allow the NGB to proactively monitor whether the types of stressors are changing over time.

- **Gather longitudinal data on the impacts of the full range of stress prevention and mitigation programs on workforce stressors.** Leaders in our discussions talked about the many formal and informal programs in place to help personnel address their day-to-day stress, which results from not only the increased OPTEMPO and PERSTEMPO but also the stressors of everyday life. While there are many programs, it might be useful for leadership to better understand which programs are most successful at helping reduce stress when people do access them and why, and which (if any) might be failing to reach part of their target audience and why. Ideally, longitudinal data on mental health outcomes, as well as undocumented (e.g., self-reported individual and family) stress would be measured and tracked over time. These data, along with detailed information about what services people access when faced with stress and why, would be important to include and track as well. Because our study was limited in scope, we were not able to do a deep dive into the impacts and reach of these programs. It is possible that longitudinal data demonstrating the effectiveness of some of the programs exists already.

- **Improve service member access to care and well-being services and supports.**
  - **Address child care access as a stressor.** Leaders view child care access as an important added stressor for a key subset of the National Guard workforce. We recommend three activities. First, conduct a survey and focus groups to define the range of child care issues that personnel are facing and gather ideas for solutions. Second, hold discussions with SMEs to explore any state-specific complications. Third, use existing personnel data to define the key demographics of interest (e.g., members with children at varying ages) and prevalence by state to better understand how many guard members and others are potentially affected by these issues.
  - **Identify pros and cons of solutions to address health care access issues and gaps in coverage.** Leaders talked at length about the limitations of TRICARE and about gaps in coverage that occur between activations. We recommend that the NGB undertake a study to identify different courses of action (COAs) that could help close some of these coverage and access gaps or mitigate their effects on both readiness and stress on the force. We recommend that the study consider COAs that fall within the existing ability of the NGB to execute (e.g., enhanced communication with the Defense Health Agency and TRICARE service providers), as well as COAs that might require changes by Congress to implement (e.g., ways to incentivize better provider participation, increased online health care access, improving continuity of care over statuses, and ways to support continual preventive care when Guard members are not activated). Examination of the pros and cons should consider the costs of the various options (e.g., impacts on recruiting and retention and stress on members and families). This research effort should also consider stopgap COAs because many ideal policy solutions—even if approved—might take a long time to fully implement. We are aware of a study already underway that is designed to look at these health care options for the NGB. We offer these as starting ideas to consider in that study or in future studies on the topic.
  - **Understand and address interpersonal disconnectedness.** Leaders noted that the workforce might feel more disconnected than in past years because of longer commute distances, more remote work and training, and the COVID-19 pandemic. This potential anonymity of service resulting from a sense of disconnection could represent a significant stressor negatively affecting service members' sense of well-being and willingness to continue to serve. Such disconnectedness could reduce the workforce's support network and make it harder for leaders in the field to recognize when the individual Guard members whom they supervise are facing personal hardships,

challenges, or other stressors. We recommend conducting a study to explore this issue further and would include at least two approaches. The first would be to use personnel data to explore whether the typical distance between people's homes and their drill locations and assignments has, in fact, changed over time and how that might vary by state. The second would be to field a survey to explore and document the extent to which connectedness is actually a concern of many detachment leaders and members of the force. In addition, the survey would ideally explore views on the problems that might result from disconnectedness (in cases where it exists), identify new ways to remedy or mitigate those problems, and assess attitudes toward some existing ideas that leaders might want to consider (e.g., enhanced leadership training and increased online access to connect with units and other service members).

- **Track and mitigate PERSTEMPO.**
  - **Better track and account for state-workload PERSTEMPO stressors.** Currently, there is no systematic way for federal activation, training, or assignment decisions to take into consideration whether individuals have recently been tasked with high workloads at the state level. Without information on the full demands being placed on service members, leaders cannot take steps to make accommodations or exceptions for individuals who need them. This lack of information also makes it difficult for NGB leaders to establish policies and programs to address workload stressors. It would be ideal for the NGB, in close conjunction with the states, to develop a dashboard tool to help leaders regularly gather information about workloads at the state level. Such a tracking mechanism would provide the basis for conversation among NGB leaders, the states, and service leaders about long-term impacts of state-workload stressors, whether on PERSTEMPO or other areas like readiness.
  - **Explore whether existing processes for defining National Guard staffing requirements (at both the state and federal level) are capturing and addressing fluctuations in workload demands.** In our discussions, leaders said that from 2020 onward, some demands—particularly at the state level and in some states—appear to have been higher than in past years. The limited scope of this study prevented us from exploring in detail whether the National Guard has a process in place to systematically document these increased demands and adjust its staffing requirements and allocations in response. However, given that the increased demands are viewed by leadership as potentially putting stress on the workforce, reviewing how staffing requirements are set and whether the process could be improved to be more responsive to OPTEMPO fluctuations is one way to help mitigate this stress. We therefore recommend that the NGB, in close coordination with the U.S. Army and U.S. Air Force leadership, engage with TAGs to review the system in place to determine whether it can proactively capture and address these fluctuations in demand (including how long they are sustained, whether they are federal or state-level demands, and how they vary by state and over time). We recommend including in that examination a review of the process

that feeds information back to governors and NGB leaders, as well as to the services that ultimately allocate manpower based on validated military requirements. This could inform adjustments to how Guard personnel are allocated across the states and whether changes to staffing requirements for certain occupations might be needed to better account for the demands on a force that is vital for the nation's security.

Closing Thoughts

It is likely that the various stressors discussed in this report are affecting different parts of the force in varying ways. Similarly, each of the possible follow-on inquiries could provide useful insights to help address stressors for certain subsets of personnel. However, no single effort will likely reduce stressors for all personnel. If pockets of personnel continue to face stressors, over time, those groups might become resentful because their concerns have not been addressed. Including a review of the potential benefits and impacts across key demographic subgroups (e.g., gender, race, or prior active component) will be especially important to ensuring key pockets of personnel do not feel neglected.

Communicating widely about the studies and efforts that the NGB decides to undertake might also be beneficial. Even if solutions take years to be fully realized, the NGB can benefit from establishing a line of research that shows members of the workforce that leadership is committed to understanding their issues and finding solutions. Continued studies, such as those described above, can help ensure that all NGB personnel feel valued and are ready to support the United States in whatever ways they are called on to do so in the future. Ultimately, the National Guard's ongoing ability to defend and serve the states and the country will rely on the initiatives and investments the NGB makes to address those stressors and support its people.

More Details on National Guard Health Care Coverage Options by Status

In Chapter 6, we discussed health care issues that result from changes in duty status and provided a brief summary table outlining health care options by status. Here, we provide a more-detailed summary of the options available (both health and dental care) under each type of status and the general timing for qualifying and receiving benefits under each. The text found in the following box, which is pulled directly from the Military OneSource website, shows the complexity of options available.

Description of National Guard Health Care Coverage Options by Status

On military duty for 30 days or less: Service members may qualify to purchase TRI-CARE Reserve Select, a premium-based, voluntary health plan that provides comprehensive health coverage for the sponsor and family. Traditional drilling National Guard and reserve members are eligible for the TRICARE Reserve Select health plan. The service member may also qualify for Line of Duty Care for any injury or illness sustained in the line of duty, including traveling to and from the place of duty. For dental care, the sponsor and family can enroll in the TRICARE Dental Program. You will enroll separately and pay separate monthly premiums.

Activated for more than 30 consecutive days: When the service member is activated (called or ordered to active duty for more than 30 consecutive days under federal orders), the service member becomes eligible for the same health and dental benefits as active-duty service members. The service member will enroll in one of the following Prime options upon arrival at the final duty station:

- TRICARE Prime
- TRICARE Prime Remote
- TRICARE Prime Overseas
- TRICARE Prime Remote Overseas.

If the service member is enrolled in the TRICARE Dental Program when called to active duty, the coverage is automatically terminated. The service member is now covered by active-duty dental benefits and receives dental care at military dental treatment facilities and through the TRICARE Active Duty Dental Program.

The service member's family becomes eligible for the same TRICARE benefits as active-duty family members when the service member is on active duty for more than 30 consecutive days. The family can use any of the following plans depending on where they live when the service member is activated:

- TRICARE Prime
- TRICARE Prime Remote
- TRICARE Standard and Extra
- TRICARE Prime Overseas
- TRICARE Prime Remote Overseas
- TRICARE Standard Overseas
- US Family Health Plan
- TRICARE Young Adult (for dependent adult children up to age 26).

If the service member's family is enrolled in the TRICARE Dental Program, their coverage continues uninterrupted and their premiums are reduced to the "active duty family member" rates. If not already enrolled, they can enroll in the TRICARE Dental Program at any time.

Pre-activation or "early" eligibility: If the service member is issued delayed-effective-date active-duty orders for more than 30 consecutive days in support of a contingency operation, Guard and reserve members may qualify up to 180 days early for active-duty TRICARE benefits. This "pre-activation benefit" begins on the date the orders are issued but not earlier than 180 days before reporting to active duty.

During the pre-activation period, service members are covered as "active-duty service members" and receive active-duty medical and dental benefits. Eligible family members are covered as "active duty family members" and can enroll in one of TRICARE's Prime options or use TRICARE Standard and Extra.

The service personnel office will tell members if they are eligible for pre-activation benefits when they receive their delayed-effective-date active-duty orders. If the service member does not meet these "early eligibility" requirements, your coverage (and your family's coverage) will begin on the first day of the service member's orders.

When deactivated: When the service member leaves active duty, or deactivates, the family's health plan options may be different if the service member was called to active duty in support of a contingency operation. If activated in support of a contingency operation:

- Sponsor is immediately covered by the Transitional Assistance Management Program for 180 days. TAMP coverage begins on the first day after leaving active-duty service. Family members are also covered during the TAMP period.
- After TAMP ends, service members may qualify to purchase TRS for personal and family coverage.
- If service members don't qualify for TRS, another option is to purchase the Continued Health Care Benefit Program.
- Service members continue to be covered under active-duty dental benefits during TAMP. After TAMP ends, TRICARE Dental Program coverage will automatically resume (if previously enrolled) and monthly premiums will resume until the 12-month minimum enrollment period is reached.
- If the service member's family is enrolled in the TRICARE Dental Program, their coverage continues uninterrupted, however, their premium payments will revert back to their original rates.

If the service member was not activated in support of a contingency operation, the family does not qualify for TAMP, and active-duty benefits (including dental) end immediately.

SOURCE: Military OneSource, 2023.

Abbreviations

COA	course of action
COVID-19	coronavirus disease 2019
DoD	U.S. Department of Defense
NGB	National Guard Bureau
OPTEMPO	operational tempo
PERSTEMPO	personnel tempo
SME	subject-matter expert
TAG	The Adjutant General
TRS	TRICARE Reserve Select
VA	Veterans Affairs

References

Avey, James B., Fred Luthans, and Susan M. Jensen, "Psychological Capital: A Positive Resource for Combating Employee Stress and Turnover," *Human Resource Management*, Vol. 48, No. 5, September 28, 2009.

Beynon, Steve, "The National Guard Is Having a Nightmarish Time Keeping Soldiers and Recruiting New Ones," Military.com, September 22, 2022. As of August 7, 2023:
https://www.military.com/daily-news/2022/09/22/
national-guard-having-nightmarish-time-keeping-soldiers-and-recruiting-new-ones.html

Beynon, Steve, "Army National Guard Can't Retain Enough Soldiers, Even as Active Duty Meets Goals," Military.com, June 22, 2023. As of November 7, 2023:
https://www.military.com/daily-news/2023/06/22/
army-national-guard-cant-retain-enough-soldiers-even-active-duty-meets-goals.html

ChildCare Aware of America, "Air Force Fee Assistance," webpage, undated-a. As of November 7, 2023:
https://www.childcareaware.org/fee-assistancerespite/military-families/air-force/fee-assistance/
#howfeeassist

ChildCare Aware of America, "Army National Guard Weekend Drill Child Care (WDCC) Program," webpage, undated-b. As of May 19, 2023:
https://www.childcareaware.org/fee-assistancerespite/military-families/army/arngwdcc/

Colligan, Thomas W., and Eileen M. Higgins, "Workplace Stress: Etiology and Consequences," *Journal of Workplace Behavioral Health*, Vol. 21, No. 2, 2006.

Cunningham, Lucretia, "Child Care Remains a Challenge for Drilling Guardsmen," *Reserve + National Guard Magazine*, December 17, 2021.

Edú-Valsania, Sergio, Ana Laguía, and Juan A. Moriano, "Burnout: A Review of Theory and Measurement," *International Journal of Environmental Research and Public Health*, Vol. 19, No. 3, 2022.

Elsea, Jennifer, *The Posse Comitatus Act and Related Matters: The Use of the Military to Execute Civilian Law*, Congressional Research Service, R42659, updated November 6, 2018.

Florida Department of Corrections, "FDC Partners with Florida National Guard to Supplement Staffing at Select Correctional Institutions," press release, September 9, 2022.

Goh, Joel, Jeffrey Pfeffer, and Stefanos A. Zenios, "The Relationship Between Workplace Stressors and Mortality and Health Costs in the United States," *Management Science*, Vol. 62, No. 2, 2016.

Hardison, Chaitra M., Carl Rhodes, Jacqueline A. Mauro, Lindsay Daugherty, Erin Gerbec, and Craig Ramsey, *Identifying Key Workplace Stressors Affecting Twentieth Air Force: Analyses Conducted from December 2012 Through February 2013*, RAND Corporation, RR-592-AF, 2014. As of May 19, 2023:
https://www.rand.org/pubs/research_reports/RR592.html

Hardison, Chaitra M., Eyal Aharoni, Christopher Larson, Steven Trochlil, and Alexander C. Hou, *Stress and Dissatisfaction in the Air Force's Remotely Piloted Aircraft Community: Focus Group Findings*, RAND Corporation, RR-1756-AF, 2017. As of November 7, 2023:
https://www.rand.org/pubs/research_reports/RR1756.html

Hokanson, Daniel R., "2022 National Guard Bureau Posture Statement," testimony before the U.S. Senate Defense Appropriations Subcommittee, May 18, 2021.

Hokanson, Daniel R., "A Review of the President's FY2023 Funding Request and Budget Justification for the National Guard and Reserve," testimony before the U.S. Senate Defense Appropriations Subcommittee, June 7, 2022.

Hokanson, Daniel R., and Tony L. Whitehead, "Chief of the National Guard Bureau Army Gen. Daniel R. Hokanson and Senior Enlisted Advisor to the Chief Tony L. Whitehead Hold a Press Briefing," U.S. Department of Defense, January 24, 2023.

Kamarck, Kristy, "Defense Primer: Personnel Tempo (PERSTEMPO)," Congressional Research Service, IF11007, version 11, November 23, 2022.

Kapp, Lawrence, *Defense Primer: Reserve Forces*, Congressional Research Service, IF10540, updated January 17, 2023.

Kapp, Lawrence, and Barbara Salazar Torreon, *Reserve Component Personnel Issues: Questions and Answers*, Congressional Research Service, RL30802, updated November 2, 2021.

Knowles, Hannah, and Karoun Demirjian, "Omicron Slammed Essential Workers. So the National Guard Became Teachers, Janitors and More," *Washington Post*, February 18, 2022.

Military Childcare, homepage, undated. As of November 7, 2023:
https://public.militarychildcare.csd.disa.mil/mcc-central/mcchome#/

Military OneSource, "A Benefits Guide for National Guard and Family Members," webpage, February 21, 2023. As of April 27, 2023:
https://www.militaryonesource.mil/national-guard/national-guard-family-program/benefitsguide/#:~:text=Traditional%20drilling%20National%20Guard%20and,from%20the%20place%20of%20duty

My Air Force Benefits, "Child Development Centers (CDCs), Air National Guard: State Active Duty," benefit fact sheet, webpage, May 25, 2022. As of May 19, 2023:
https://www.myairforcebenefits.us.af.mil/Benefit-Library/Federal-Benefits/Child-Development-Centers-(CDCs)?serv=22

My Air Force Benefits, "Child Care Fee Assistance Programs, Air National Guard: State Active Duty," benefit fact sheet, webpage, March 3, 2023. As of May 19, 2023:
https://www.myairforcebenefits.us.af.mil/Benefit-Library/Federal-Benefits/Child-Care-Fee-Assistance-Programs?serv=22

Nierenberg, Amelia, "The National Guard Deploys to Classrooms," *New York Times*, February 23, 2022.

Texas Military Department, "Operation Lone Star," webpage, undated. As of May 25, 2023:
https://tmd.texas.gov/border

TRICARE, *TRICARE Choices for National Guard and Reserve*, handbook, U.S. Department of Defense, May 2022.

U.S. Code, Title 10, Armed Forces.

U.S. Code, Title 10, Sections 251–255, Insurrection.

U.S. Code, Title 18, Section 1385, Use of Army and Air Force as Posse Comitatus.

U.S. Code, Title 32, National Guard.

U.S. House of Representatives, National Defense Authorization Act for Fiscal Year 2018, Report 115–404, November 9, 2017.

U.S. Secret Service, "National Special Security Events Credentialing," webpage, undated. As of May 19, 2023:
https://www.secretservice.gov/protection/events/credentialing

Ware, Doug G., "Air National Guard Expects Staffing Deficit of up to 4,000 This Year, General Says," *Stars and Stripes*, May 30, 2023.

West Virginia National Guard, "W.Va. Guard to Provide Support to Dept. of Corrections to Alleviate Staffing Shortages," press release, August 12, 2022. As of November 7, 2023:
https://www.wv.ng.mil/News/Article/3126771/
wva-guard-to-provide-support-to-dept-of-corrections-to-alleviate-staffing-short/